7 Things God Hates
By Julia Anshasi

Giant Publishing Company
Lincoln, Nebraska, USA

2024 by Julia Anshasi

Published by Giant Publishing Company
Post Office Box 6455
Lincoln, NE 68506
www.giantpublishingcompany.com

Printed in the United States of America

All rights reserved. No part of this publication may be used or reproduced in any form or by any electronic or mechanical means, including information storage and retrieval systems, without permission in writing from the publisher.

All scripture quotations are from the King James Version of the Bible, unless otherwise noted.

Library of Congress Cataloging-in-Publication Data
Anshasi, Julia, 1963 -
7 Things God Hates   Theology/Julia Anshasi
   1. Christianity
   2. Theology

ISBN 979-8-9898098-0-6
TX0009391645

These six things the LORD hates,
Yes, seven are an abomination to Him:
A proud look,
A lying tongue,
Hands that shed innocent blood,
A heart that devises wicked plans,
Feet that are swift in running to evil,
A false witness who speaks lies,
And one who sows discord among brethren.
Proverbs 6: 16 – 19 (New King James Version)

Books by Julia Anshasi

Broken ~ Poems from the Holy Spirit
Copyright 2017 – Winner of the 2021 Illumination Book Awards Silver Medal

Some Things are HOT! Some Things are NOT!
Copyright 2018

Behind the Word: Bible Stories to Ignite Your Imagination
Copyright 2018

Why Did the Dinosaurs Die?
Copyright 2019

Winter in Eden
Copyright 2020 – Winner of the 2022 Illumination Book Awards Bronze Medal

The Revelation of Jesus Christ
Copyright 2020

One Part Nonsense
Copyright 2020

Books by Julia Anshasi, continued

Spiritual Exhaustion
Copyright 2021 - Winner of the 2022 Illumination Book Awards Silver Medal

Forgiving Yourself
Copyright 2021

Lame for Life
Copyright 2022

Quiet ~ A devotional
Copyright 2022

Unbearable Loneliness
Copyright 2024

The Cult I Left
Copyright 2025

Table of Contents

Introduction

Chapter 1: A proud look……………..……Page 9

Chapter 2: A lying tongue……….…........Page 29

Chapter 3: Hands that shed
 innocent blood……………...Page 47

Chapter 4: A heart that devises
 wicked plans………………..Page 59

Chapter 5: Feet that are swift in
 running to evil……………...Page 75

Chapter 6: A false witness who
 speaks lies…………….…....Page 85

Chapter 7: One who sows discord
 among brethren…………....Page 95

Chapter 8: The body, redeemed…………Page 103

Introduction

There are many, many Christian denominations. From Catholics and Episcopalians, to Baptists and Pentecostals, from mainline denominations to small home churches that no one has heard of, each one has its own method of worshipping God. Many churches have a mission statement, or a "we believe" message on their websites, explaining what their particular emphasis is. Each group would claim to love and serve God.

As a child who grew up in church, and as an adult who lives daily as a part of my local church, I have seen one thing that all churches have in common: they are full of sinful people. As the saying goes, there is no perfect church, and if you find one, don't attend there, because you will ruin it.

Now that I have fewer years ahead of me than behind me, I realize more than ever the importance of the church aligning herself with God's agenda, God's plan, God's desires, and God's heart. If God loves something, we must love that thing as well. If God hates something, we must hate it as well.

Does God really hate anything? After all, God is love, isn't He?

This book will attempt to show the reader that yes, God does hate, and if the believer wants to align himself with God's heart, he or she must also determine to hate the things that God hates. ~ Julia Anshasi

Chapter 1: A proud look

Pride is number one on the list of things that God hates. Not murder, not rape or pedophilia. Pride.

Why?

Pride is what made Heylel, the most beautiful angel, become Satan. Heylel is unfortunately translated as Lucifer in the King James Bible.

How art thou fallen from heaven, O Lucifer, son of the morning! how art thou cut down to the ground, which didst weaken the nations! Isaiah 14: 12

Few people refer to Satan as Heylel, because very few know that that was the name that God gave him.

There are four angels mentioned in particular in the Bible: the Angel of the LORD, who is a pre-incarnate appearance of Jesus Christ, Gabriel, who brought messages to Daniel, Zachariah, and Mary, Michael, who helped Gabriel and who fights alongside the church against Satan, and Heylel, Satan himself. Here are some verses where these angels are mentioned.

And the angel of the LORD appeared unto (Moses) in a flame of fire out of the midst of a bush: and he looked, and, behold, the bush burned with fire, and the bush was not consumed. Exodus 3: 2

And I heard a man's voice between the banks of Ulai,

which called, and said, Gabriel, make this man to understand the vision. Daniel 8: 16

And in the sixth month the angel Gabriel was sent from God unto a city of Galilee, named Nazareth... Luke 1: 26

But the prince of the kingdom of Persia withstood me one and twenty days: but, lo, Michael, one of the chief princes, came to help me; and I remained there with the kings of Persia. Daniel 10: 13

And there was war in heaven: Michael and his angels fought against the dragon; and the dragon fought and his angels... Revelation 12: 7

The suffix "el" which appears at the end of the names Gabriel, Michael, and Heylel, simply means God. It is from a root Hebrew word meaning "might, strength, or power."

Gabriel means "man of God." Michael means "who is like God?" Heylel means "the morning star."

The translation of Heylel as Lucifer is extremely unfortunate. Heylel is a Hebrew word, and Lucifer is a Latin word. Lucifer means "full of light," or, "carrying the light," in Latin.

And no marvel; for Satan himself is transformed into an angel of light. 2 Corinthians 11: 14

The original languages of the Bible we use today are Aramaic, Hebrew, and Greek – not Latin.

It is not just God's holy angels who have names ending in "el."

And he said, Thy name shall be called no more Jacob, but Israel: for as a prince hast thou power with God and with men, and hast prevailed. Genesis 32: 28

Israel means "prince of God."

And he said unto me, O Daniel, a man greatly beloved, understand the words that I speak unto thee, and stand upright: for unto thee am I now sent. And when he had spoken this word unto me, I stood trembling. Daniel 10: 11

Daniel means "judge of God."

And Jacob called the name of the place Peniel: for I have seen God face to face, and my life is preserved. Genesis 32: 30

Peniel means "face of God."

And Jacob called the name of the place where God spake with him, Bethel. Genesis 35: 15

Bethel means "house of God."

And the child Samuel grew on, and was in favour both with the LORD, and also with men. 1 Samuel 2: 26

Samuel means "heard of God."

The word of the LORD came expressly unto Ezekiel the priest, the son of Buzi, in the land of the Chaldeans by the river Chebar; and the hand of the LORD was there upon him. Ezekiel 1: 3

Ezekiel means "God will strengthen."

But this is that which was spoken by the prophet Joel... Acts 2: 16

Joel means "Jehovah is his God."

God created Heylel to be a perfect, shining, morning star who would reflect God's glory. Reflecting God's glory is the also the purpose of the church. The church of God does not have any glory of her own, but is designed to reflect the brilliance and brightness of God.

God gave us an illustration of this in His creation. The sun is so bright that no one can look at it. If you try, you will be blinded. The sun is light itself. The moon, on the other hand, has no inherent light. There should be no way we can see the moon from Earth. But we can. The moon, a dead ball of rock and dust, reflects the sun. Scientifically, this is impossible.

Jesus Christ is referred to as the sun throughout the Bible.

But unto you that fear my name shall the Sun of righteousness arise with healing in his wings; and ye shall go forth, and grow up as calves of the stall. Malachi 4: 2

And (Jesus) was transfigured before them: and his face did shine as the sun, and his raiment was white as the light. Matthew 17: 2

We have also a more sure word of prophecy; whereunto ye do well that ye take heed, as unto a light that shineth in a dark place, until the day dawn, and the day star arise in your hearts... 2 Peter 1: 19

The sun is the only star we can see during the day. Hence, it is the day star – Jesus Christ.

And (Jesus) had in his right hand seven stars: and out of his mouth went a sharp twoedged sword: and his countenance was as the sun shineth in his strength. Revelation 1: 16

Immediately after the tribulation of those days shall the sun be darkened, and the moon shall not give her light, and the stars shall fall from heaven, and the powers of the heavens shall be shaken... Matthew 14: 29

Even though it is impossible for any human being to extinguish the light of Jesus Christ, He (the Sun) will choose to be darkened temporarily after the tribulation. The moon (the church) will not reflect His glory during that time, because His glory will be temporarily darkened.

And the sun was darkened, and the veil of the temple was rent in the midst. Luke 23: 45

When Jesus was crucified, the natural sun high up in the atmosphere could not shine. He is a natural counterpart to the spiritual Sun, Jesus Christ.

And God said, Let there be light: and there was light. Genesis 1: 3

This Light was created on the first day of creation, before God created the natural sun in our atmosphere, on the fourth day (Genesis 1: 16).

That was the true Light, which lighteth every man that cometh into the world. John 1:9

For the stars of heaven and the constellations thereof shall not give their light: the sun shall be darkened in his going forth, and the moon shall not cause her light to shine. Isaiah 13: 10

The sun shall be turned into darkness, and the moon into blood, before the great and terrible day of the LORD come. Joel 2: 31

The sun shall be turned into darkness, and the moon into blood, before the great and notable day of the Lord come... Acts 2: 20

The church will be martyred (turned into blood) before the day of the Lord.

The stars are little suns. They have their own internal sources of light. That's why we can see them from Earth.

There is one glory of the sun, and another glory of the moon, and another glory of the stars: for one star differeth from another star in glory. 1 Corinthians 15: 41

The stars represent believers, or angels, in the Bible.

When the morning stars sang together, and all the sons of God shouted for joy? Job 38: 7

He telleth the number of the stars; he calleth them all by their names. Psalm 147: 4

Praise ye him, sun and moon: praise him, all ye stars of light. Psalm 148: 3

And they that be wise shall shine as the brightness of the firmament; and they that turn many to righteousness as the stars for ever and ever. Daniel 12: 3

Fallen stars are believers or angels who have fallen from grace.

And it waxed great, even to the host of heaven; and it cast down some of the host and of the stars to the ground, and stamped upon them. Daniel 8: 10

And the stars of heaven shall fall, and the powers that are in heaven shall be shaken. Mark 13: 25

Raging waves of the sea, foaming out their own shame; wandering stars, to whom is reserved the blackness of darkness for ever. Jude 1: 13

And the stars of heaven fell unto the earth, even as a fig tree casteth her untimely figs, when she is shaken of a mighty wind. Revelation 6: 13

And the third angel sounded, and there fell a great star from heaven, burning as it were a lamp, and it fell upon the third part of the rivers, and upon the fountains of waters; And the name of the star is called Wormwood: and the third part of the waters became wormwood; and many men died of the waters, because they were made bitter. Revelation 8: 10 - 11

And his tail drew the third part of the stars of heaven, and did cast them to the earth... Revelation 12: 4a

The natural stars that we see up in the sky at night could never fall and land on the earth. If even one star did that, the earth would be burned to annihilation. The physical planet Earth that we all live on would exist no more.

God is a God of light.

This then is the message which we have heard of him, and declare unto you, that God is light, and in him is no darkness at all. 1 John 1: 5

God is not a mixture of light and darkness. Once again, the natural world shows us this. When you walk into a dark room and turn on the light switch, the darkness disappears instantly. It doesn't move slowly out of the room, or remain in patches here and there. It is simply gone.

Heylel was created as a being of light. He reflected God's glory. But he wasn't satisfied with simply reflecting glory. He wanted to have all of God's glory for himself. He wanted to be like God. He wasn't satisfied with his name - Morning Star. He wanted to be Elohim - Creator, Mighty and Strong. He wanted to be El Elyon – The Most High God. He wanted to be El Shaddai – God Almighty.

For thou hast said in thine heart, I will ascend into heaven, I will exalt my throne above the stars of God: I will sit also upon the mount of the congregation, in the sides of the north: I will ascend above the heights of the clouds; I will be like the most High. Isaiah 14: 13 - 14

Heylel was created to be very beautiful.

Thine heart was lifted up because of thy beauty, thou hast corrupted thy wisdom by reason of thy brightness: I will cast thee to the ground, I will lay thee before kings, that they may behold thee. Ezekiel 28: 17

And (Jesus) said unto them, I beheld Satan as lightning fall from heaven. Luke 10: 18

And this is why God hates pride so much.

The pride of thine heart hath deceived thee, thou that dwellest in the clefts of the rock, whose habitation is high; that saith in his heart, Who shall bring me down to the ground? Though thou exalt thyself as the eagle, and though thou set thy nest among the stars, thence will I bring thee down, saith the LORD. Obadiah 3: 3-4

Whatever good things you and I have, we have them because God gave them to us. If I am physically beautiful, I am beautiful because God made me beautiful. If I am brilliant, kind, generous, wealthy, or have any other positive attributes, I am those things because He made me those things.

The arrogance of mankind is simply astounding. Someone may go to school and earn a PhD, and then start strutting around like a peacock, thinking he is now smarter than everyone else. Who gave you that brain that enabled you to go to school and study, little man?

I remember a few years back, a very public feud between two country music bands. They traded lots of insults back and forth. One stated that the other didn't have the right to criticize him, because that band did not have anywhere near the song-writing capabilities that he had.

The man who made that prideful claim died of cancer.

Pride is a stench in God's nostrils. It is a slap in the face to Him. He will not tolerate it.

Pride goeth before destruction, and an haughty spirit before a fall. Proverbs 16: 18

If a person is full of pride, make no mistake, he will fall. God will topple him from his puny man-made pedestal.

King Nebuchadnezzar is a very good example of this.

In Daniel chapter 3, we read that king Nebuchadnezzar had a statue made of himself that was ninety feet tall. It was made of gold.

Imagine the cost of a ninety-foot gold statue of yourself. It may have been just gold-plated, and not solid gold, but the Bible doesn't say that, so we can't know for sure. Either way, spending that much money on an image of yourself is extremely prideful. But it gets worse.

Then an herald cried aloud, To you it is commanded, O people, nations, and languages, That at what time ye hear the sound of the cornet, flute, harp, sackbut, psaltery, dulcimer, and all kinds of musick, ye fall down and worship the golden image that Nebuchadnezzar the king hath set up: And whoso falleth not down and worshippeth shall the same hour be cast into the midst of a burning fiery furnace. Daniel 3: 4 - 6

The king gave a commandment to kill anyone who refused to worship the gold statue of himself.

This is something beyond pride. It is the same thing that Heylel suffered from. A psychologist would call it a God complex.

To kill someone who refuses to worship you is an extreme reaction, to say the least.

Three people refused to worship the statue: Shadrach, Meshach, and Abednego. And Nebuchadnezzar made good on his threat.

Then these men were bound in their coats, their hosen, and their hats, and their other garments, and were cast into the midst of the burning fiery furnace. Daniel 3: 21

God rewards faith. He rewards those who refuse to buckle under the pressure of evil governments and rulers.

But without faith it is impossible to please him: for he that cometh to God must believe that he is, and that he is a rewarder of them that diligently seek him. Hebrews 11: 6

Then Nebuchadnezzar the king was astonished, and rose up in haste, and spake, and said unto his counsellors, Did not we cast three men bound into the midst of the fire? They answered and said unto the king, True, O king. He answered and said, Lo, I see four men loose, walking in the midst of the fire, and they have no hurt; and the form of the fourth is like the Son of God. Daniel 3: 24 - 25

Jesus Christ Himself showed up and walked with the three Hebrew men in the midst of the fire. His presence would not allow the fire to burn them.

After this miraculous rescue, you would think that Nebuchadnezzar would have learned his lesson. And he did, but only for a short time.

Therefore I (Nebuchadnezzar) *make a decree, That every people, nation, and language, which speak any thing amiss against the God of Shadrach, Meshach, and Abednego, shall be cut in pieces, and their houses shall be made a dunghill: because there is no other God that can deliver after this sort.* Daniel 3: 29

This incident was a warning to the king – don't let pride invade your heart! But in the very next chapter of Daniel, God had to give Nebuchadnezzar another warning. He gave him a dream about a tree being cut down. Daniel interpreted the dream for the king.

This is the interpretation, O king, and this is the decree of the most High, which is come upon my lord the king: That they shall drive thee from men, and thy dwelling shall be with the beasts of the field, and they shall make thee to eat grass as oxen, and they shall wet thee with the dew of heaven, and seven times shall pass over thee, till thou know that the most High ruleth in the kingdom of men, and giveth it to whomsoever he will. Daniel 4: 24 - 25

God warned Nebuchadnezzar that if he didn't turn away from his pride, the punishment would be severe. He would live as an animal for seven years, with no human reasoning. He would lose his mind! It would take that long for him to know that God is the One who has ultimate rule on earth, and God is the One who decides who will rule in any earthly kingdom, not man, and certainly not Nebuchadnezzar.

Nebuchadnezzar didn't heed the warning. A year later, he in fact did lose his mind.

All this came upon the king Nebuchadnezzar. At the end of twelve months he walked in the palace of the kingdom of Babylon. The king spake, and said, Is not this great Babylon, that I have built for the house of the kingdom by the might of my power, and for the honour of my majesty? While the word was in the king's mouth, there fell a voice from heaven, saying, O king Nebuchadnezzar, to thee it is spoken; The kingdom is departed from thee. Daniel 4: 28 - 31

Just as God had warned him, and just as Daniel had interpreted his dream a year before, Nebuchadnezzar lost his mind while he was still congratulating himself for his beautiful kingdom. He became insane, left the palace, lived in the wilderness, ate grass, and didn't get a haircut or cut his nails for seven years.

Let another man praise thee, and not thine own mouth; a stranger, and not thine own lips. Proverbs 27: 2

We have all heard people bragging about their accomplishments, their jobs, their money, their education, their looks, their children, and on and on. No one can stand to listen to this, and yet so many people do it. If listening to someone bragging is like nails on a chalkboard, why not make an effort to recognize it in yourself, and immediately silence yourself?

Nebuchadnezzar came back to his senses seven years later. Obviously, pride was very deeply rooted within him, if God had to use seven years of insanity to humble him.

God hates pride! He will use insanity if He has to, or severe illness if necessary, to humble a prideful person. This is what happened to Miriam.

Miriam was Moses' sister. Moses was the greatest leader the people of Israel had ever had. As such, he was a target of jealousy. When a person is jealous of someone else, pride easily rears its ugly head, as in:

He's not so great. I can do what he does. I can probably do it even better!

In Numbers chapter 12, we read how Miriam and Aaron became jealous of Moses.

And they said, Hath the LORD indeed spoken only by Moses? hath he not spoken also by us? And the LORD heard it. And the LORD came down in the pillar of the cloud, and stood in the door of the tabernacle, and called Aaron and Miriam: and they both came forth. And he said, Hear now my words: If there be a prophet among you, I the LORD will make myself known unto him in a vision, and will speak unto him in a dream. My servant Moses is not so, who is faithful in all mine house. With him will I speak mouth to mouth, even apparently, and not in dark speeches; and the similitude of the LORD shall he behold: wherefore then were ye not afraid to speak against my servant Moses? And the anger of the LORD was kindled against them; and he departed. Numbers 12: 2, 5 - 9

You and I should be afraid to speak against God's servants! The Lord Himself says so. But too many people are not afraid. They openly criticize God's preachers, evangelists, prophets, and more. This is very prevalent among those in the ministry. I cringe whenever I hear a well-known Christian figure criticizing another. Even if you are not well-known, don't do this! God will deal with our brothers and sisters in Christ; it is not our place to do so.

Miriam found this out the hard way.

And the cloud departed from off the tabernacle; and, behold, Miriam became leprous, white as snow: and Aaron looked upon Miriam, and, behold, she was leprous. Numbers 12: 10

God, being the merciful God that He is, healed Miriam of leprosy seven days later. But the lesson remained.

Remember what the LORD thy God did unto Miriam by the way, after that ye were come forth out of Egypt. Deuteronomy 24: 9

God is telling us to remember what happened to Miriam! The next time you or I feel that we can hear from God better, preach better, or generally perform better than our brother or sister, let's stop and remember Miriam. I don't know about you, but I don't want leprosy or insanity.

Pride is so prevalent! We find it throughout the Bible.

And there was also a strife among (the twelve disciples), *which of them should be accounted the greatest. And* (Jesus) *said unto them, The kings of the Gentiles exercise lordship over them; and they that exercise authority upon them are called benefactors. But ye shall not be so: but he that is greatest among you, let him be as the younger; and he that is chief, as he that doth serve. For whether is greater, he that sitteth at meat, or he that serveth? is not he that sitteth at meat? but I am among you as he that serveth.* Luke 22: 24 – 27

I wonder if Jesus was amused or saddened by His twelve squabbling disciples as He heard, "I'm greater than you are! No, I'm greater than you are!" Maybe He was a little of both. He told them that in order to be great, they must learn to be servants. And He is the greatest example of a servant that the world has ever known. Almighty God, lowering Himself to take on the form of a human being, to die for the sins of the world. What an outstanding example of humility, and the absolute antithesis of pride.

And whosoever shall exalt himself shall be abased; and he that shall humble himself shall be exalted. Matthew 23: 12

Don't wait for God to humble you. Humble yourself. If God has to do it, it will not be pretty, and you will wish that you had not forced Him to discipline you.

You don't even need to act in a prideful way to be guilty of the sin of pride. The verse that we are studying states that God hates "a proud look." You can belittle someone, or insult someone, without saying a word.

Many of us remember middle school or high school, when the cool kid that we wanted to be friends with simply gave us "a look" as we walked by, and that look said more than a hundred words. I have seen this look many times!

You poor thing. Your clothes are out of style. Your hair looks terrible. You're not even on the basketball/ volleyball/ soccer team, because you're a klutz. I feel so sorry for you. Please keep walking; I don't want anyone to think that I am actually talking to someone like you.

I have had to repent many times of giving that look to another person. May God help us.

Each one of us has been fearfully and wonderfully made (Psalm 139: 14), each with our own gifts and talents. We have absolutely no right to look down upon another person.

Every one that is proud in heart is an abomination to the LORD: though hand join in hand, he shall not be unpunished. Proverbs 16: 5

Chapter 1 references

Strong's Exhaustive Concordance of the Bible with Hebrew and Greek Lexicons
Hebrew4Christians.com
Online-Latin-dictionary.com
Bibleportal.com

Chapter 2: A lying tongue

The first lie recorded in the Bible is in Genesis chapter three, verses four and five. After God told Adam not to eat from the tree of the knowledge of good and evil, Satan showed up with a lie.

And the serpent said unto the woman, Ye shall not surely die: For God doth know that in the day ye eat thereof, then your eyes shall be opened, and ye shall be as gods, knowing good and evil.

Satan lied to Eve and told her it would be no problem if she did what God had told mankind not to do.

This is always Satan's strategy.

The second lie recorded in the Bible is in Genesis chapter four, verse nine.

And the LORD said unto Cain, Where is Abel thy brother? And he said, I know not: Am I my brother's keeper?

Of course Cain knew where Abel was; he had just killed him. And of course Cain knew that God knew what he had done, but he lied about it anyway.

No one has to teach a child to lie; he does it naturally. It starts when we are tiny children with cookie crumbs on our faces – "No Mommy; I didn't eat a cookie." It continues on as we blame our siblings for something that we ourselves did. Some of us get really good at lying – so much so that we even convince ourselves that we are not lying.

Lying is a demonic spirit. The devil is the originator of all lies.

Ye are of your father the devil, and the lusts of your father ye will do. He was a murderer from the beginning, and abode not in the truth, because there is no truth in him. When he speaketh a lie, he speaketh of his own: for he is a liar, and the father of it. John 8: 44

Whenever I am tempted to lie, I ask myself if Satan is my father. This really helps to put the brakes on my lies.

Lies are extremely damaging. They wreak havoc in relationships.

In Genesis chapter twelve, we read about a stunning lie that Abram (Abraham) told about his wife. To save his own skin, he convinced Sarai (Sarah) to tell people that she was his sister.

Therefore it shall come to pass, when the Egyptians shall see thee, that they shall say, This is his wife: and they will kill me, but they will save thee alive. Say, I pray thee, thou art my sister: that it may be well with me for thy sake; and my soul shall live because of thee. Genesis 12: 12 - 13

Wasn't God the One who originally told Abram to leave his home (Genesis 12: 1)? Wasn't God well able to preserve Abram's life, if He was the One who sent him on this journey in the first place?

Now the LORD had said unto Abram, Get thee out of thy country, and from thy kindred, and from thy father's house, unto a land that I will shew thee... Genesis 12: 1

Yes, God was the One. But Abram thought it would be best to tell a lie about Sarai, so they did. This didn't turn out well.

The princes also of Pharaoh saw her, and commended her before Pharaoh: and the woman was taken into Pharaoh's house. Genesis 12: 15

Had Abram really stopped to think ahead of time what might happen if everyone thought Sarai was his sister? What actually did happen was, he was separated from her. She went into the palace, and Abram remained outside. I wonder if Abram thought about what was going on inside Pharaoh's palace.

And the LORD plagued Pharaoh and his house with great plagues because of Sarai Abram's wife. And Pharaoh called Abram and said, What is this that thou hast done unto me? why didst thou not tell me that she was thy wife? Why saidst thou, She is my sister? so I might have taken her to me to wife: now therefore behold thy wife, take her, and go thy way. Genesis 12: 17 - 19

These verses imply that Pharaoh did not sleep with Sarai. But the question arises: would Abram have minded if he had?

Lies have consequences!

Abram didn't learn from this experience. He lied again later, and it was the same lie.

And Abraham said of Sarah his wife, She is my sister: and Abimelech king of Gerar sent, and took Sarah. But God came to Abimelech in a dream by night, and said to him, Behold, thou art but a dead man, for the woman which thou hast taken; for she is a man's wife. But Abimelech had not come near her: and he said, LORD, wilt thou slay also a righteous nation? Said he not unto me, She is my sister? and she, even she herself said, He is my brother: in the integrity of my heart and innocency of my hands have I done this. Then Abimelech called Abraham, and said unto him, What hast thou done unto us? and what have I offended thee, that thou hast brought on me and on my kingdom a great sin? thou hast done deeds unto me that ought not to be done. And Abraham said, Because I thought, Surely the fear of God is not in this place; and they will slay me for my wife's sake. Genesis 20: 2 – 5, 9, 11

Once again, this could have had disastrous consequences. God Himself prevented Abimelech from touching Sarah.

How did Sarah feel about these lies? The Bible doesn't tell us, but I can imagine that she was frightened at the prospect of being forced to become someone else's wife, and resentful toward her husband for putting her in such a dangerous position.

God designed the man to be the protection and covering of the woman. By telling these lies about Sarah, Abraham in effect threw her to the wolves and told her she was on her own. This was a great betrayal of her trust, but we know that Abraham and Sarah remained together. They somehow managed to overcome the lies and move on.

I strongly doubt that Abraham told his son Isaac about the lies he had told about his mother. Yet we find Isaac doing the very same thing.

And Isaac dwelt in Gerar: And the men of the place asked him of his wife; and he said, She is my sister: for he feared to say, She is my wife; lest, said he, the men of the place should kill me for Rebekah; because she was fair to look upon. And it came to pass, when he had been there a long time, that Abimelech king of the Philistines looked out at a window, and saw, and, behold, Isaac was sporting with Rebekah his wife. And Abimelech called Isaac, and said, Behold, of a surety she is thy wife; and how saidst thou, She is my sister? And Isaac said unto him, Because I said, Lest I die for her. Genesis 26: 6 - 9

This Abimelech may have been the son of the Abimelech mentioned in Genesis 20. Or, Abimelech may have been his title as one of the kings of the Philistines, as Pharaoh was the title of the kings of Egypt. It is doubtful that the two kings that were lied to by Abraham and his son were the same person.

Regardless, both father and son told the same lie to a king.

Fear caused Abraham and Isaac to lie about their wives. Jealousy also causes people to lie. We read about this in 1 Kings 13.

This is a very sad story. An unnamed man of God was sent by God to Bethel to pronounce judgment, which he did. The Lord had told him before he went not to eat or drink while he was there. He did everything the Lord had told him to do, and then left town. After he left, an old prophet who lived there went after him.

The old prophet caught up with the young man of God, and invited him back to his house. At first, the young man refused.

And he said, I may not return with thee, nor go in with thee: neither will I eat bread nor drink water with thee in this place: For it was said to me by the word of the LORD, *Thou shalt eat no bread nor drink water there, nor turn again to go by the way that thou camest. He said unto him, I am a prophet also as thou art; and an angel spake unto me by the word of the LORD, saying, Bring him back with thee into thine house, that he may eat bread and drink water. But he lied unto him.* 1 Kings 13: 16 - 18

There are so many things at play in this story. The young man had clear instructions from God, which he followed. But then an older prophet gave him opposite instructions. As you read this story, you can almost hear the young man wavering.

Well, God, I know you told me not to eat or drink while I was there, but this man has been a prophet a lot longer than I have been. I really should respect his word and do what he says. It would be rude to refuse, wouldn't it? You must have spoken to him and given him a different word for me than what you gave to me directly.

Red flag warning! God speaks to each one of us. He does not speak only through one person who is somehow more holy than we are. The young man had clear instructions from God, which he ended up disobeying, because he was intimidated by an older, wiser prophet.

This is a completely different scenario than the story of Aaron and Miriam criticizing Moses behind his back. God had designated Moses as the prophet of Israel, and God spoke to him face to face. Everyone in Israel knew this. Aaron and Miriam criticized Moses because they were jealous of him, not because he was failing in his role as prophet.

In 1 Kings 13, the Bible doesn't tell us the old prophet's motivation for lying to the young man, but once again jealousy seems to be the clear reason to me.

Sometimes people lie because they desperately want to hold on to what they have. The old prophet may have thought he was losing his office of prophet to a younger man, and would do anything, including lying, to hold onto that office. But the gift of prophecy is from God. It cannot be retained by lying.

For the gifts and calling of God are without repentance. Romans 11: 29

Whatever God has given you and me, He will never take back. The old prophet was not losing his gift of prophecy! Those of us who have been in the church for a long time must make way for younger people to step in and assume their roles in the church. Jealousy must never enter into this.

The young man succumbed to the old prophet's pressure, and went back to his house with him.

And it came to pass, as they sat at the table, that the word of the LORD came unto the prophet that brought him back: And he cried unto the man of God that came from Judah, saying, Thus saith the LORD,

Forasmuch as thou hast disobeyed the mouth of the LORD, and hast not kept the commandment which the LORD thy God commanded thee, But camest back, and hast eaten bread and drunk water in the place, of the which the Lord did say to thee, Eat no bread, and drink no water; thy carcase shall not come unto the sepulchre of thy fathers. 1 Kings 13: 20 - 22

There is no hint of repentance in the old prophet's words. Never once does he say, "I'm sorry I lied to you and caused you to disobey the Lord."

And this is why God hates lying so much.

And whosoever shall offend one of these little ones that believe in me, it is better for him that a millstone were hanged about his neck, and he were cast into the sea. Mark 9: 42

A little one is not just a child! A little one is anyone who is younger in faith, has been walking with the Lord for a shorter time, is not quite as "spiritual" as you are, or is more gullible than you are. Offending that person does not simply mean saying something offensive. Offending him or her often means leading that person down a path of destruction.

The old prophet, through his lies, directly caused the death of the young man.

And it came to pass, after he had eaten bread, and after he had drunk, that he saddled for him the ass, to wit, for the prophet whom he had brought back. And when he was gone, a lion met him by the way, and slew him: and his carcase was cast in the way, and the ass stood by it, the lion also stood by the carcase. 1 Kings 13: 23 – 24

I have seen firsthand the deadly results of lying in my own family. Someone who holds a grudge against another person spreads vicious lies against him or her, causing others in the family to turn against that person. This divides the family, and people don't speak to one another any longer, literally for years. And even worse, when the liar is confronted, he worsens the effect of the original lies by saying he "has no idea" why family members aren't speaking to one another.

Why does this happen? Because of jealousy.

And the prophet took up the carcase of the man of God, and laid it upon the ass, and brought it back: and the old prophet came to the city, to mourn and to bury him. And he laid his carcase in his own grave; and they mourned over him, saying, Alas, my brother! And it came to pass, after he had buried him, that he spake to his sons, saying, When I am dead, then bury me in the sepulchre wherein the man of God is buried; lay my bones beside his bones... 1 Kings 13: 29 – 31

After his words literally killed the young prophet, the old prophet finally seemed to be repentant over what he had done.

Death and life are in the power of the tongue...
Proverbs 18: 21a

Perhaps, as he stood looking down on the lifeless body of the young man, the old prophet was convicted of his sin of lying. I hope so.

There is certainly a cautionary tale in all of this for you and me. Don't believe everything you hear.

Beloved, believe not every spirit, but try the spirits whether they are of God: because many false prophets are gone out into the world. 1 John 4: 1

I believe a false prophet is, in many cases, one who was once a true prophet who succumbs to pride, jealously, greed, or some other sin. This person eventually becomes less and less interested in hearing a true word from God, and more and more interested in receiving admiration from men.

Remember, God will not withdraw the gift of prophecy from someone He has given it to. But He also will never override our free will. This is how hearing from the Holy Spirit gets twisted into listening to lying spirits.

Why do people lie? Usually, it is to save their own skins. But sometimes people lie for no reason. I have known people who lie about everything, all the time. No one is accusing them of anything, or confronting them about anything, yet they lie anyway, about the most inconsequential and trivial matters. As I stated before, this is a demonic spirit.

And for this cause God shall send them strong delusion, that they should believe a lie... 2 Thessalonians 2: 11

There is no such thing as a little white lie, or a lie that doesn't matter. God takes lying very seriously.

In the book of Acts, we read about the early church – this group of believers who turned the world upside down. These people were so in tune with God and with each other, they made the decision to jointly own everything they had.

And the multitude of them that believed were of one heart and of one soul: neither said any of them that ought of the things which he possessed was his own; but they had all things common. Acts 4: 32

Can you imagine a church today that is so filled with the Holy Spirit, that no one owns a car, or a pair of shoes, or a bank account? Everything that anyone has is free for anyone in the church to use.

Neither was there any among them that lacked: for as many as were possessors of lands or houses sold them, and brought the prices of the things that were sold, And laid them down at the apostles' feet: and distribution was made unto every man according as he had need. Acts 4: 34 - 35

Until lying entered in.

But a certain man named Ananias, with Sapphira his wife, sold a possession, And kept back part of the price, his wife also being privy to it, and brought a certain part, and laid it at the apostles' feet. But Peter said, Ananias, why hath Satan filled thine heart to lie to the Holy Ghost, and to keep back part of the price of the land? Whiles it remained, was it not thine own? and after it was sold, was it not in thine own power? why hast thou conceived this thing in thine heart? thou hast not lied unto men, but unto God. And Ananias hearing these words fell down, and gave up the ghost: and great fear came on all them that heard these things. Acts 5: 1 - 5

I can imagine! If someone told a lie, then dropped dead in front of you, you would also be filled with fear.

For the wages of sin is death; but the gift of God is eternal life through Jesus Christ our Lord. Romans 6: 23

This is a dramatic illustration of a liar receiving his "wages" immediately. Later, we read of Ananias' wife also dropping dead when confronted by the Apostle Peter about the lie (Acts 5: 10).

God hates lies! I cringe when I hear parents telling children that if they are good, Santa Claus will bring them presents. By all means, tell your children about Santa if you wish, in the same way you would tell them about Cinderella or Jack and the Beanstalk, but please don't lie to them!

Be not deceived; God is not mocked: for whatsoever a man soweth, that shall he also reap. Galatians 6: 7

Parents, listen to me. If you lie to your children when they are little, they will lie to you when they are teenagers. If you sow seeds of deception in your children when they are young, you will reap a crop of lies. Don't do it.

In 2 Kings 5 we see another account of a lie with disastrous consequences. Naaman, a Syrian general, came to the prophet Elisha for healing of leprosy. Elisha gave him instructions on how to be healed, and Naaman (very reluctantly) followed them. And he was healed! Naaman was so grateful, he wanted to give Elisha a gift, but Elisha refused, and Naaman went on his way. Elisha's servant, Gehazi, overheard this conversation and followed Naaman, concocting a crafty lie in order to receive a gift for himself.

...My master hath sent me, saying, Behold, even now there be come to me from mount Ephraim two young men of the sons of the prophets: give them, I pray thee, a talent of silver, and two changes of garments. 2 Kings 5: 22b

Gehazi was apparently short on cash, and wanted some new clothes, so he decided to trick Naaman into giving him the things he wanted, by lying to him and telling him that Elisha wanted them.

Naaman urged Gehazi to take two talents of silver, not the one talent that he had asked for. So Gehazi left with his gifts and went back home to Elisha. He probably thought the situation had turned out really well for him. But Elisha, being a prophet, had seen the whole encounter in the spiritual realm.

And (Elisha) said unto him, Went not mine heart with thee, when the man turned again from his chariot to meet thee? Is it a time to receive money, and to receive garments, and oliveyards, and vineyards, and sheep, and oxen, and menservants, and maidservants? The leprosy therefore of Naaman shall cleave unto thee, and unto thy seed for ever. And (Gehazi) went out from his presence a leper as white as snow. 2 Kings 5: 26 - 27

Too many people have lied to get money, get a job, get a wife or a husband, or any number of things. But lies are always discovered!

...be sure your sin will find you out. Numbers 32: 23b

Gehazi lived the rest of his life as a leper - not only he, but his descendants forever.

In today's political landscape, it is extremely rare to find a politician who *doesn't* lie. Lying seems to be as commonplace as breathing. This is not the practice of one particular political party! A poster I saw once put it so clearly. Under a picture of a dead elephant and a dead donkey, the caption read: "They're all liars."

Political liars never seem to realize that their lies will be found out. This is baffling and also somewhat amusing. As far back as I can remember, every sitting president has been caught in a lie of some sort. Yet politicians continue to lie in order to get re-elected. After they are in office, they do whatever is most advantageous for them, not the people who elected them.

Yes, our votes are important, but God is the One who ultimately decides who will hold office.

Daniel answered and said, Blessed be the name of God for ever and ever: for wisdom and might are his: And he changeth the times and the seasons: he removeth kings, and setteth up kings: he giveth wisdom unto the wise, and knowledge to them that know understanding: He revealeth the deep and secret things: he knoweth what is in the darkness, and the light dwelleth with him. Daniel 2: 20 – 22

God always reveals the deep and secret things. He always knows what is hidden in the darkness, and He always brings it to light.

Therefore whatsoever ye have spoken in darkness shall be heard in the light; and that which ye have spoken in the ear in closets shall be proclaimed upon the housetops. Luke 12: 3

Let's make sure that our words are true. Lies cannot stand the light of God's truth – it exposes them, and they wither away.

Lies are the property of the devil. Leave them with him.

Remove from me the way of lying: and grant me thy law graciously. Psalm 119: 29

Chapter 2 references

Gotquestions.org

Chapter 3: Hands that shed innocent blood

In the previous chapter, we read about how Cain lied to God regarding his brother's whereabouts. He lied because he had murdered him.

And Cain talked with Abel his brother: and it came to pass, when they were in the field, that Cain rose up against Abel his brother, and slew him. Genesis 4: 8

Cain hated Abel because God accepted Abel's sacrifice, and rejected his. His hatred of his own brother culminated in murder.

God created blood to carry life throughout our bodies. Without blood, there is no life.

For the life of the flesh is in the blood: and I have given it to you upon the altar to make an atonement for your souls: for it is the blood that maketh an atonement for the soul. Leviticus 17: 11

God sees our blood as very precious.

And (God) said, What hast thou done? the voice of thy brother's blood crieth unto me from the ground. Genesis 4: 10

I don't believe this is a mere figure of speech. I believe that when innocent blood is shed, the blood literally cries out to God.

And surely your blood of your lives will I require; at the hand of every beast will I require it, and at the hand of man; at the hand of every man's brother will I require the life of man. Genesis 9: 5

Before Jesus Christ died on the cross, the life of all of humanity was required to be redeemed with an animal sacrifice.

And almost all things are by the law purged with blood; and without shedding of blood is no remission. Hebrews 9: 22

It seems an obvious statement, but there is a difference between innocent blood and guilty blood.

Whoso sheddeth man's blood, by man shall his blood be shed: for in the image of God made he man. Genesis 9: 6

While debating the death penalty with a young woman in my church, I tried to get the point across that capital punishment was simply the natural consequence of murder. Does God enjoy seeing people killed? No. Is God delighted when murderers die? No. Does capital punishment satisfy the requirements of God's law? Yes.

God made man in His image. We are truly blessed, because no other creature on earth bears the image of God.

And this is why God hates the shedding of innocent blood so much.

The murderer who is executed in prison is experiencing the natural consequences of committing murder. And I think I can confidently say that the families and friends of the murder victims feel no happiness when the execution occurs. The only thing they feel is a sense of justice served, and the closing of a door.

God is the life-giver. He is the only One who can create and originate life. Each human being is engraved with His image, so the shedding of innocent blood and the stamping out of that life is a grave sin.

In 2 Samuel 11 - 12, we read the very sad story of King David's fall into adultery and murder.

David was a man after God's own heart. The prophet Samuel told the previous king, Saul, this very thing, when he came to him and told him that God had rejected him.

But now thy kingdom shall not continue: the LORD *hath sought him a man after his own heart, and the* LORD *hath commanded him to be captain over his people, because thou hast not kept that which the* LORD *commanded thee.* 1 Samuel 13: 14

God removed Saul from being king, and replaced him with David, a man after God's own heart. This expression simply means that David yearned to follow God, and wanted to follow Him more than anything else. It doesn't mean that David's heart was like God's heart, which a lot of people seem to believe - that is impossible.

The heart is deceitful above all things, and desperately wicked: who can know it? Jeremiah 17:9

David committed adultery with Uriah's wife. When she told him she was pregnant, he tried to manipulate the situation to make Uriah think that the baby was his. When that didn't work, he ordered Uriah to be killed.

And (David) wrote in the letter, saying, Set ye Uriah in the forefront of the hottest battle, and retire ye from him, that he may be smitten, and die. 2 Samuel 11: 15

Uriah's only crime was refusing to sleep with his wife while his fellow soldiers were out fighting for Israel. For this, he died at the king's order.

God sent Nathan the prophet to speak to David about what he had done.

Wherefore hast thou despised the commandment of the LORD, to do evil in his sight? thou hast killed Uriah the Hittite with the sword, and hast taken his wife to be thy wife, and hast slain him with the sword of the children of Ammon. Now therefore the sword shall never depart from thine house; because thou hast despised me, and hast taken the wife of Uriah the

Hittite to be thy wife. Thus saith the LORD, Behold, I will raise up evil against thee out of thine own house, and I will take thy wives before thine eyes, and give them unto thy neighbour, and he shall lie with thy wives in the sight of this sun. For thou didst it secretly: but I will do this thing before all Israel, and before the sun. 2 Samuel 12: 9 - 12

Shedding innocent blood has life-long consequences.

Because of David's actions, God told him that the sword would never depart from his house. David spent the rest of his life at war with the nations surrounding Israel, and at war with his own children. He was humiliated when his own son took his concubines to the roof of the palace, and slept with them openly, "before all Israel."

We are free to choose our own actions. God created each one of us with a free will. But we are never free to choose the consequences of our actions. More often than not, these consequences continue, long after we are gone.

Here's an example. David wanted to build a structure to house the Ark of the Covenant. God told him no.

Then David the king stood up upon his feet, and said, Hear me, my brethren, and my people: As for me, I had in mine heart to build an house of rest for the ark of the covenant of the LORD, and for the footstool of our God, and had made ready for the building: But

God said unto me, Thou shalt not build an house for my name, because thou hast been a man of war, and hast shed blood. 1 Chronicles 28: 2 – 3

We know that Uriah was an innocent man, not deserving to die in the way that David had plotted. There may have been other innocent blood that David had shed; we don't know. But because of this, David was not allowed to build a house for the Ark. Solomon, his son, had the honor of doing that. David's actions disqualified him from doing what he wanted to do.

When we shed innocent blood, the consequences are generational. It never stops with the person committing the act; the consequences carry on to his or her descendants.

The LORD is longsuffering, and of great mercy, forgiving iniquity and transgression, and by no means clearing the guilty, visiting the iniquity of the fathers upon the children unto the third and fourth generation. Numbers 14: 18

Who is more innocent than Jesus Christ? He was betrayed, His innocent blood was shed, and the consequences of that were severe.

When Judas, who had betrayed him, realized that Jesus had been condemned to die, he was filled with remorse. So he took the thirty pieces of silver back to the leading priests and the elders. "I have sinned," he declared, "for I have betrayed an innocent man." "What do we care?" they retorted. "That's your problem." Then Judas threw the silver coins down in the Temple and went out and hanged himself. Matthew 27: 3 – 5, NLT

The King James Version of this account records Judas as saying, "I have betrayed the innocent blood."

Judas' actions are recorded in the Psalms, hundreds of years before they occurred.

Set thou a wicked man over him: and let Satan stand at his right hand. When he shall be judged, let him be condemned: and let his prayer become sin. Let his days be few; and let another take his office. Let his children be fatherless, and his wife a widow. Psalm 109: 6 - 9

The Bible tells us nothing about Judas' wife and children, but after he hanged himself, they were indeed widowed and fatherless. His wife and children suffered because of his actions, no doubt unto the "third and fourth generation."

Judas lost his position as one of the original twelve apostles, and another took his place.

Remember that as much as God hates the shedding of innocent blood, Satan loves it.

According to The Satanic Temple, as a part of one's religious beliefs, innocent blood must be shed. It is common practice for Satanists to sacrifice animals and humans during their rituals, and they do not flinch at sacrificing an unborn baby.

How do Satanists sacrifice unborn babies? By suing states that seek to minimize or eliminate abortion, by fighting for free and unrestricted abortions, and by attempting to cloak the murder of unborn babies as free exercise of religion.

In the United States, all religions are not created equal. In states that have passed laws requiring a pregnant woman to view an ultrasound of her baby before having an abortion, Satanists have put forth the legal argument that the very sight of an unborn baby on ultrasound violates their religious beliefs. These legal challenges have not been upheld. Contrary to what those on the political left keep saying, America was founded on Judeo-Christian beliefs. This is blindingly obvious in the first part of the second sentence of our Declaration of Independence:

We hold these Truths to be self-evident, that all Men are created equal, that they are endowed by their Creator with certain unalienable Rights, that among these are Life, Liberty, and the Pursuit of Happiness...

This is what I learn from reading this part of the Declaration:

Number 1: We are created.
Number 2: We have a Creator.
Number 3: Our Creator gave us rights.
Number 4: Among the rights He gave us is the right to life.

As has been said many times, if I am not alive, none of my other rights matter.

It's very interesting to me that the courts have not recognized Satanists' "right" to murder. The courts do not recognize such a right, because our judicial system was built upon Judeo-Christian principles. Therefore, the religion of satanic worship is not given the same credence as other religious faiths in this country (yet).

Taking a human life should never be done lightly. This is why murderers on death row are granted many appeals before they are executed. When the day of execution comes, there should be no doubt in anyone's mind that justice has been served, and the blood shed was not innocent.

But what if an innocent person is executed by the State? We would be naïve to think that this has never happened. My take on that is this: God knows that the person is innocent, and God will judge the actions of those who carried out the execution. If the evidence was faulty, and the execution was done deliberately anyway, that is called murder, and those people will be judged accordingly. If the execution was done because all the evidence (wrongly) convicted an innocent person, then that is called a mistake, and those responsible will be judged differently.

Innocent people die every day because of mistakes, and it is horrible. Doctors administer the wrong drug to a patient in the hospital, and that person dies. Someone accidentally hits another person with his car, and that person is killed.

I read an account of a soldier who was ordered to open fire on a group of children standing in the road in front of her tank. She obeyed the order, but she never recovered mentally or emotionally from that incident.

As Christians, we know that God forgives our sins and our mistakes, even the shedding of innocent blood, if we ask Him to. Thank God He does.

This I recall to my mind, therefore have I hope. It is of the LORD's *mercies that we are not consumed, because his compassions fail not. They are new every morning: great is thy faithfulness.* Lamentations 3: 21 - 23

God is faithful. He has great compassion on you and me. He is full of mercy toward us.

Be merciful, O LORD, *unto thy people Israel, whom thou hast redeemed, and lay not innocent blood unto thy people of Israel's charge. And the blood shall be forgiven them.* Deuteronomy 21: 8

Our world is becoming more violent by the day. More and more innocent blood is being shed. Basic human compassion has diminished to the point of being almost non-existent.

And because iniquity shall abound, the love of many shall wax cold. Matthew 24: 12

Today, if you express a political opinion that is different than your neighbor's, you risk getting a punch in the face.

May God help us.

The murderer rising with the light killeth the poor and needy, and in the night is as a thief. Job 24: 14

Chapter 4: A heart that devises wicked plans

The name Jezebel is synonymous with wickedness. I don't read in the Bible one good thing that that woman did. She was the wife of Ahab, king of Israel, and she pulled the strings, and almost completely controlled her husband.

She started her reign of wickedness by killing most of God's prophets.

And Ahab called Obadiah, which was the governor of his house. (Now Obadiah feared the LORD greatly: For it was so, when Jezebel cut off the prophets of the LORD, that Obadiah took an hundred prophets, and hid them by fifty in a cave, and fed them with bread and water.) 1 Kings 18: 3 - 4

What better way to silence the voice of God than by killing His prophets? But God cannot be silenced.

Thank God for Obadiah. He saved some of the true prophets by hiding them in a cave. The prophet Elijah also survived Jezebel's execution order, and he turned the tables on her. He told Ahab to gather all of Jezebel's false prophets together in one place.

Now therefore send, and gather to me all Israel unto mount Carmel, and the prophets of Baal four hundred and fifty, and the prophets of the groves four hundred, which eat at Jezebel's table. 1 Kings 18: 19

If Ahab had thought about this for even a minute, he would have seen that this was a God-trap. But he didn't.

Elijah ended up killing all of the false prophets of Baal (1 Kings 18: 40). And Jezebel was not happy.

And Ahab told Jezebel all that Elijah had done, and withal how he had slain all the prophets with the sword. Then Jezebel sent a messenger unto Elijah, saying, So let the gods do to me, and more also, if I make not thy life as the life of one of them by to morrow about this time. 1 Kings 19: 1 - 2

No doubt Jezebel was angry that she had missed Elijah when she was ordering the slaying of the prophets. She quickly began plotting Elijah's death.

Jezebel's wicked plan did not succeed. Elijah left town, and Jezebel soon turned her attention to others who she felt were standing in her way.

Ahab wanted to take possession of Naboth's vineyard, and he was very unhappy when Naboth said no.

And Ahab came into his house heavy and displeased because of the word which Naboth the Jezreelite had spoken to him: for he had said, I will not give thee the inheritance of my fathers. And he laid him down upon his bed, and turned away his face, and would eat no bread. But Jezebel his wife came to him, and said unto him, Why is thy spirit so sad, that thou eatest no bread? And he said unto her, Because I spake unto Naboth the Jezreelite, and said unto him, Give me thy vineyard for money; or else, if it please thee, I will give thee another vineyard for it: and he answered, I will not give thee my vineyard. And Jezebel his wife said unto him, Dost thou now govern the kingdom of Israel? arise, and eat bread, and let thine heart be merry: I will give thee the vineyard of Naboth the Jezreelite. 1 Kings 21: 4 - 7

Translated, this means that Jezebel believed that she could have whatever she wanted, because she was the queen of Israel, and it didn't matter what anyone else wanted. It also didn't matter if innocent people had to die in order for her to get what she wanted – she was the queen, and what the queen wants, the queen gets.

It's interesting to me that Ahab didn't insist on taking Naboth's vineyard by force. That was all Jezebel's idea. She quickly devised another wicked plan.

So she wrote letters in Ahab's name, and sealed them with his seal, and sent the letters unto the elders and to the nobles that were in his city, dwelling with Naboth. And she wrote in the letters, saying, Proclaim a fast, and set Naboth on high among the people: And set two men, sons of Belial, before him, to bear witness against him, saying, Thou didst blaspheme God and the king. And then carry him out, and stone him, that he may die. 1 Kings 21: 8 – 10

It happened just as Jezebel planned. Naboth, an innocent man, was stoned to death so that Ahab could get his vineyard.

The Bible doesn't say anywhere that Ahab disagreed with his wife's wicked plans. He just went along with them, like a dog on a leash.

The spirit of Jezebel is very prevalent. Although when we think of Jezebel, we think of a woman, a man can also carry the Jezebel spirit. That spirit is always plotting against other people, always trying to pull down and destroy others, so that she/he can have what they have. The spirit of Jezebel is very much a spirit of jealousy and control.

***

It is a special kind of evil to plot against another person. In the book of Judges, we read the sad story of a man of God, whose downfall was women. They plotted and connived against him.

Samson was a person whom God had chosen to judge Israel. He was extremely gifted and very intelligent, but his gifts and intelligence were no match for the women he became entangled with.

The first plot recorded against Samson came from the Philistines, in Judges, chapter fourteen. Samson planned to marry a Philistine woman, against his parents' wishes. The Philistines threatened her and her family with death, if she didn't trick Samson into revealing the answer to a riddle that he had put to them.

Never mind that the Philistines had readily agreed to the terms of the riddle. If they couldn't solve it, they were supposed to give Samson thirty sheets and thirty garments. They originally agreed to these terms, then changed their minds when they couldn't solve the riddle.

And it came to pass on the seventh day, that they said unto Samson's wife, Entice thy husband, that he may declare unto us the riddle, lest we burn thee and thy father's house with fire: have ye called us to take that we have? is it not so? Judges 14: 15

The Philistines plotted to burn Samson's betrothed wife and her family if she couldn't get the answer to the riddle. She manipulated the information out of Samson with tears and nagging – the Jezebel spirit at work once again. But Samson killed thirty Philistine men, took their clothing, and gave it to the men who had "solved" the riddle (after his wife-to-be gave them the answer). He fulfilled the terms that he had laid out at the beginning, in a way that none of the Philistines saw coming.

He that diggeth a pit shall fall into it; and whoso breaketh an hedge, a serpent shall bite him. Ecclesiastes 10: 8

If you are devising a wicked plan against someone else, don't be surprised when the evil you planned for that person turns around and bites you.

Samson's wife-to-be was given in marriage by her father to someone else. Samson found this out when he went to visit her. He retaliated against the Philistines by burning all their crops (Judges 15: 5). They plotted one type of revenge after another against him, but because the Lord was with him, none of their plots worked, and he slaughtered thousands of them.

Next, the Gazites plotted to kill Samson.

Then went Samson to Gaza, and saw there an harlot, and went in unto her. And it was told the Gazites, saying, Samson is come hither. And they compassed him in, and laid wait for him all night in the gate of the city, and were quiet all the night, saying, In the morning, when it is day, we shall kill him. Judges 16: 1-2

The Gazites didn't succeed, either. Imagine lying in wait all night, plotting to kill someone, only to have him rip the gates of your city off their hinges and carry them away (verse three). I think after witnessing that, they hastily abandoned their wicked plan.

As I stated before, Samson had a great weakness for women, which was his downfall.

And it came to pass afterward, that he loved a woman in the valley of Sorek, whose name was Delilah. And the lords of the Philistines came up unto her, and said unto her, Entice him, and see wherein his great strength lieth, and by what means we may prevail against him, that we may bind him to afflict him; and we will give thee every one of us eleven hundred pieces of silver. Judges 16: 4 - 5

Samson's weakness was Delilah, and Delilah's weakness was money. As we read the very sad story of what happened to Samson in Judges chapter sixteen, we see a man who connected with the wrong woman, we see evil people who plotted to kill him, or at least, to maim him, and we see a heartless, selfish woman who saw the opportunity to make a lot of money, and grabbed ahold of it with both hands.

As before, Samson was manipulated by a woman (this time, Delilah), into giving away a secret that he should have kept to himself. It resulted in permanent physical blindness (verse twenty-one), and temporary spiritual blindness.

After the Philistines made Samson into their personal court jester, he found himself in the house of Dagon, an idol's temple. He stood between two pillars that held the house up, and made a decision.

And Samson took hold of the two middle pillars upon which the house stood, and on which it was borne up, of the one with his right hand, and of the other with his left. And Samson said, Let me die with the Philistines. And he bowed himself with all his might; and the house fell upon the lords, and upon all the people that were therein. So the dead which he slew at his death were more than they which he slew in his life. Judges 16: 29 - 30

God had set Samson up as a judge of Israel, and he judged them for twenty years (verse thirty-one). He could have judged Israel for many more years, but he died an untimely death. But those who had plotted against him, died along with him. This is a case of God having the last laugh.

***

In the book of Nehemiah, we read how Nehemiah decided to rebuild the broken wall of Jerusalem. God was one-hundred percent behind this project, so of course His enemies did all they could to try to stop it. When Sanballat and Tobiah heard that Nehemiah had gathered men to begin the work on the wall, they immediately began plotting against him by trying to intimidate him into stopping the work.

But when Sanballat the Horonite, and Tobiah the servant, the Ammonite, and Geshem the Arabian, heard it, they laughed us to scorn, and despised us, and said, What is this thing that ye do? will ye rebel against the king? Nehemiah 2: 19

Sometimes other people's laughter is all it takes for us to abandon our God-given assignments.

Nehemiah had no intention of rebelling against the king, but Sanballat and his cronies made fun of him and his project, thinking they could discourage him and get him to stop the work.

Nehemiah had a large crew of men working. They did not let the mocking laughter stop them. They just ignored it and kept working.

But it came to pass, that when Sanballat heard that we builded the wall, he was wroth, and took great indignation, and mocked the Jews. And he spake before his brethren and the army of Samaria, and said, What do these feeble Jews? will they fortify themselves? will they sacrifice? will they make an end in a day? will they revive the stones out of the heaps of the rubbish which are burned? Now Tobiah the Ammonite was by him, and he said, Even that which they build, if a fox go up, he shall even break down their stone wall. Nehemiah 4: 1 - 3

I see the spirit of Jezebel very much at work here. Sanballat and Tobiah laughed at the Jews, mocked them, made fun of them, and discounted their work as if it was nothing. Imagine building a stone wall, and someone telling you that if a fox jumped on it, it would crumble. Their intention was to discourage the builders, but it didn't work. In my opinion, everyone had received a supernatural strength from God to work and complete the wall.

But it came to pass, that when Sanballat, and Tobiah, and the Arabians, and the Ammonites, and the Ashdodites, heard that the walls of Jerusalem were made up, and that the breaches began to be stopped, then they were very wroth, And conspired all of them together to come and to fight against Jerusalem, and to hinder it. Nehemiah 4: 7 – 8

Another wicked plan was put into place. Since laughter and mocking didn't work, Sanballat and Tobiah decided to fight. But God was one step ahead of them, as He always is. The workers knew what was about to happen, and they stationed lookouts all along the wall as it was under construction, to watch for any enemies that might be coming along. They worked with one hand, and held a weapon with the other hand.

Nehemiah finished the construction of the wall. His enemies now switched tactics, since their previous wicked plans had failed. They sent a messenger to Nehemiah, asking him to meet with them face to face.

This is almost amusing. Have you ever had people verbally attack you, mock you, threaten you, and generally make your life miserable? Then, when they see that their tactics aren't working, they suddenly want to be your friend? This is a very common ruse of the Jezebel spirit. If you are not careful, you will fall for it.

I have experienced this in my own life. It is especially hard when the person who came against you is someone you love. It is very tempting to let your guard down and tell yourself that your attacker has changed his ways, realizes how wrong he was, and is now coming to you with a repentant spirit.

As the saying goes: Trust, but verify.

This is also very common in the political realm. It never fails to amaze me how one politician can viciously attack another, dragging him or her through the mud, and then later choose that person as a running mate.

Nehemiah refused to meet with his attackers; he knew they were up to no good. But they kept pestering him. Finally, they just made up a lie.

Then sent Sanballat his servant unto me in like manner the fifth time with an open letter in his hand; Wherein was written, It is reported among the heathen, and Gashmu saith it, that thou and the Jews think to rebel: for which cause thou buildest the wall, that thou mayest be their king, according to these words. Nehemiah 6: 5 - 6

Those that are devising wicked plans are usually under a spirit of delusion. In this case, the enemies of God could not accept that Nehemiah wanted to rebuild the wall because Jerusalem was his home, and it caused him tremendous pain to see the wall broken down. No, they thought he must have some ulterior motive, namely, that he wanted to be king.

Psychologists call this projecting. Whatever evil is in a person's heart is projected onto another, along with the false accusation that the other person is guilty of the very thing that is in the first person's heart.

Nehemiah knew how to answer his accusers.

Then I sent unto him, saying, There are no such things done as thou sayest, but thou feignest them out of thine own heart. Nehemiah 6: 8

In other words, you're making it all up.

So the wall was finished in the twenty and fifth day of the month Elul, in fifty and two days. And it came to pass, that when all our enemies heard thereof, and all the heathen that were about us saw these things, they were much cast down in their own eyes: for they perceived that this work was wrought of our God. Nehemiah 6: 15 - 16

No wicked plan of the enemy will succeed against a child of God.

***

In 2 Samuel 13, we read the story of a wicked plot that was hatched over a two-year period. Amnon and

Absalom were half-brothers, the sons of King David. Amnon raped his half-sister, Tamar, who was Absalom's full sister. Absalom began plotting his revenge.

And Absalom spake unto his brother Amnon neither good nor bad: for Absalom hated Amnon, because he had forced his sister Tamar. 2 Samuel 13: 22

Verse twenty-three starts out: *And it came to pass after two full years...*

Those who plot evil against others believe that God will not discipline or judge the wrong that has been done. They take matters into their own hands. But God does enact vengeance. He is the only One who can.

Dearly beloved, avenge not yourselves, but rather give place unto wrath: for it is written, Vengeance is mine; I will repay, saith the Lord. Romans 12: 19

Absalom waited two full years to exact vengeance upon Amnon for raping Tamar. After luring Amnon to his house for a family get-together, he put his plot into action.

Now Absalom had commanded his servants, saying, Mark ye now when Amnon's heart is merry with wine, and when I say unto you, Smite Amnon; then kill him, fear not: have not I commanded you? be courageous, and be valiant. 2 Samuel 13: 28

After getting his servants to do his dirty work for him, Absalom fled. But there is no running away from the Lord. Absalom himself died a gruesome death a few years later. After plotting to kill his own father (another plot!) Absalom's mule ran out from under him, and he was left hanging from a tree by his hair.

And (Joab) took three darts in his hand, and thrust them through the heart of Absalom, while he was yet alive in the midst of the oak. And ten young men that bare Joab's armour compassed about and smote Absalom, and slew him. 2 Samuel 18: 14b - 15

Amnon plotted to rape Tamar, and died. Absalom plotted to kill Amnon, and kill his own father, and died.

***

Perhaps the most wicked plan of all was the plan to kill Jesus Christ.

Then one of the twelve, called Judas Iscariot, went unto the chief priests, And said unto them, What will ye give me, and I will deliver him unto you? And they covenanted with him for thirty pieces of silver. And from that time he sought opportunity to betray him. Matthew 26: 14 – 16

I don't know what motivation Judas had in betraying the friend who loved him the most. Various Bible commentators have various theories. Some say that Judas was convinced Jesus would establish an earthly kingdom, and when He did, Judas would be one of His right-hand men. His betrayal of Jesus, in his mind, would force Jesus to hurry up and overthrow the Roman government and establish Himself as an earthly king. Judas just couldn't wait to get that coveted position in that earthly kingdom, so he was helping the process to move more quickly. He really didn't intend for Jesus to die.

Or, Judas simply hated Jesus, was jealous of Him, and wanted Him out of the way, and he really did want Him to die.

Or, Judas just wanted the money. Thirty pieces of silver in biblical times was roughly equivalent to half a day's wages.

We don't know Judas' motivation, but we do know that he regretted what he did. He threw the money that he had gotten down in the temple, went out, and hanged himself (Matthew 27: 3-5).

And this is why God hates so much the heart that devises wicked plans.

Just like the shedding of innocent blood, devising wicked plans doesn't end with the person who devised the plan. The consequences are passed on to many future generations.

Judas' wife was widowed, his children were fatherless, and his name has been known throughout history, to this day, as a name synonymous with treachery, betrayal, deceit, murder, injustice, back-stabbing, and any other negative adjective you can come up with.

Friends, it is simply not worth it to plot against another person. God will deal with that person. God will exact His perfect vengeance on that person; He does not need human help. No matter how justified it may seem to be, when you plot against someone else, that plot will always backfire and explode in your own face.

A good man obtaineth favour of the LORD: but a man of wicked devices will he condemn. Proverbs 12: 2

Chapter 4 references

Christianity.stackexchange.com

Chapter 5: Feet that are swift in running to evil

Solomon, the wisest man who ever lived, warned against associating with people who run to evil.

My son, walk not thou in the way with them; refrain thy foot from their path: For their feet run to evil, and make haste to shed blood. Proverbs 1: 15 - 16

What does it really mean to "run to evil?"

I think it means to be quick to participate in wrongdoing – not stopping to think about the consequences of your actions, just jumping in with both feet and taking off. In many cases, a person who is swiftly running to evil doesn't even know what is going on! I heard someone say once that if you see a crowd of people running in one direction, don't ask questions, just start running with them. This might be helpful if a fire has broken out, or if there is an active shooter, but in most circumstances, it's really in your best interest to ask a few questions before you start running.

Thou shalt not follow a multitude to do evil... Exodus 23: 2a

After Absalom, King David's son, ordered his servants to kill his half-brother Amnon, there were those who just couldn't wait to break the news to King David. But they were so quick to give him the message, they garbled it and got it all wrong.

And it came to pass, while they were in the way, that tidings came to David, saying, Absalom hath slain all the king's sons, and there is not one of them left. 2 Samuel 13: 30

David's sons had fled Absalom's party where their brother was murdered, and were fleeing back to their father. Only one of David's sons had been killed, not all of them, but the messenger didn't bother to relay the message correctly.

This is what happens when we are swift to run to evil. We don't have all the facts.

Think about the mindset of the person who was in such a hurry to get this message to the king. I wonder if this was yet another enemy of David – someone who wanted to inflict as much emotional damage as he could. If that was the case, his plan succeeded.

Then the king arose, and tare his garments, and lay on the earth; and all his servants stood by with their clothes rent. 2 Samuel 13: 31

Jonadab, David's nephew, was the evil mastermind behind Amnon's rape of his half-sister, Tamar. Now Jonadab rose gallantly to the position of truth-teller.

And Jonadab, the son of Shimeah David's brother, answered and said, Let not my lord suppose that they have slain all the young men the king's sons; for

Amnon only is dead: for by the appointment of Absalom this hath been determined from the day that he forced his sister Tamar. Now therefore let not my lord the king take the thing to his heart, to think that all the king's sons are dead: for Amnon only is dead.
2 Samuel 13: 32 - 33

You can see the spirit of Jezebel at work in Jonadab. He manipulated his cousin Amnon into raping Tamar, knowing it would infuriate Absalom. Absalom then had Amnon murdered, knowing it would hurt David. Jonadab then steps forward and gives David the message that only one of his sons is dead. He doesn't bother to tell David that none of these tragedies would have occurred without his involvement and manipulation.

The Bible doesn't tell us who gave the wrong message to David that all of his sons had been killed. But that person was swift in running to evil, and he was just plain wrong.

After Absalom was killed by Joab and his men, two men wanted to quickly run and give the news to the king. Both men knew that the king had expressly stated that no one was to harm Absalom, yet they both were very eager to be the first to tell the king his son was dead. I, personally, would not want to have that job.

Then said Ahimaaz the son of Zadok, Let me now run, and bear the king tidings, how that the LORD hath avenged him of his enemies. And Joab said unto him, Thou shalt not bear tidings this day, but thou shalt bear tidings another day: but this day thou shalt bear no tidings, because the king's son is dead. 2 Samuel 18: 19 - 20

Joab, at least, had the common sense to know that Absalom's death would not be good news to the king.

I believe that Ahimaaz' enthusiasm got the better of him. David's army had been protecting King David ever since Absalom had announced that he, not his father, was now king of Israel. Absalom was trying to kill his own father and take the throne. After Absalom's death, Ahimaaz probably thought, *"This battle is finally over. The king is safe. We can all return back to our homes, and the king can return to his palace. Let's celebrate!"*

Thankfully, Joab restrained Ahimaaz. But he was so excited, he ran anyway.

Then said Joab to Cushi, Go tell the king what thou hast seen. And Cushi bowed himself unto Joab, and ran. Then said Ahimaaz the son of Zadok yet again to Joab, But howsoever, let me, I pray thee, also run after Cushi. And Joab said, Wherefore wilt thou run, my son, seeing that thou hast no tidings ready? But howsoever, said he, let me run. And he said unto him, Run. Then Ahimaaz ran by the way of the plain, and overran Cushi. 2 Samuel 18: 21 – 23

King David was not happy when he received the news of Absalom's death.

And the king was much moved, and went up to the chamber over the gate, and wept: and as he went, thus he said, O my son Absalom, my son, my son Absalom! would God I had died for thee, O Absalom, my son, my son! 2 Samuel 18: 33

The moral of this story to me is this: What you think may be good news to someone else, may in fact be very bad news. Don't be swift to run to anyone to tell the latest thing you have heard. We need to ask the Lord for wisdom in these matters.

A fool uttereth all his mind: but a wise man keepeth it in till afterwards. Proverbs 29: 11

***

In Daniel 3, we have another example of people who were very quick to run to the king with what they thought was bad news.

After King Nebuchadnezzar set up a gigantic statue of himself, and commanded everyone to worship it, his henchmen swiftly informed him that not everyone was complying.

There are certain Jews whom thou hast set over the affairs of the province of Babylon, Shadrach, Meshach, and Abednego; these men, O king, have not regarded thee: they serve not thy gods, nor worship the golden image which thou hast set up. Daniel 3: 12

Undoubtedly, these bearers of bad news thought the king would reward them for being tattle-tales. Instead, after God miraculously rescued the three men, the king was so overwhelmed by what had happened, he promoted them.

Then the king promoted Shadrach, Meshach, and Abednego, in the province of Babylon. Daniel 3: 30

No mention is made of any promotion of the people who swiftly ran to tell the king what they certainly thought he would want to know. This is a spectacular backfire.

For among my people are found wicked men: they lay wait, as he that setteth snares; they set a trap, they catch men. Jeremiah 5: 26

Those wicked men may have temporarily caught the three Jewish men, but once again, God had the last laugh.

***

Elisha was a great prophet chosen by God. His servant Gehazi, on the other hand, was rather short-sighted. After Elisha instructed the Syrian commander, Naaman, on how to be rid of leprosy, As Naaman was leaving, he wanted to give Elisha a gift. But Elisha did not want a gift.

Gehazi, on the other hand, did want a gift. So he raced after Naaman.

But Gehazi, the servant of Elisha the man of God, said, Behold, my master hath spared Naaman this Syrian, in not receiving at his hands that which he brought: but, as the LORD liveth, I will run after him, and take somewhat of him. So Gehazi followed after Naaman. And when Naaman saw him running after him, he lighted down from the chariot to meet him, and said, Is all well? 2 Kings 5: 20 - 21

Of course, there is nothing wrong with wanting a gift from someone. I think we all do! But Elisha had specifically told Naaman that he didn't want a gift, and Gehazi had heard him say it.

Gehazi made up a story to tell Naaman that Elisha had suddenly received unexpected visitors, and now was in need of silver and clothing. Naaman ended up giving Gehazi more than he had asked for. But his plan had disastrous results.

When Gehazi returned to Elisha, after hiding his ill-gotten gifts, Elisha confronted him. Gehazi lied about where he had been and what he had done.

Elisha, being a prophet, knew exactly what had happened. He confronted Gehazi and recounted the whole story to him.

When you and I are quick to run here and there, making up stories, or spreading the latest gossip, we need to remember that God is very much aware of what we are doing. The act of running implies that a person is not stopping to think about his actions. Gehazi, of all people, should have known that Elisha would see right through his story. But greed got the best of him.

Gehazi's feet ran swiftly after Naaman, so he could get something that his boss had told him they shouldn't have. He spent the rest of his life as a leper, and his descendants were also cursed with leprosy.

***

The apostle Paul was arrested and beaten because a group of people who didn't have all the facts gathered a mob together to attack him. They had seen him in the temple, and assumed (wrongly) that he had brought a non-Jew into the temple with him (Acts 21: 27 – 29).

And all the city was moved, and the people ran together: and they took Paul, and drew him out of the temple: and forthwith the doors were shut. And as they went about to kill him, tidings came unto the chief captain of the band, that all Jerusalem was in an uproar. Acts 21: 30 - 31

Mob mentality is a frightening thing. These people literally ran to drag Apostle Paul out of the temple because of a false assumption, and most of them didn't know what he had done wrong, if anything.

And some cried one thing, some another, among the multitude: and when (the chief captain) could not know the certainty for the tumult, he commanded (Paul) to be carried into the castle. Acts 21: 34

Paul escaped a scourging by claiming his Roman citizenship, but was put into jail and remained there for a long time. Once again, this biblical narrative shows us what happens when people are swift to run to evil. In some people's minds, it doesn't even matter if an accused person is actually guilty. When the mob takes over, right and wrong go out the window.

Their feet run to evil, and they make haste to shed innocent blood: their thoughts are thoughts of iniquity; wasting and destruction are in their paths. Isaiah 59: 7

And this is why God hates so much the feet that are swift in running to evil.

It is not enough to simply run to evil, and arrive at evil as though it is a destination. It is what happens when you arrive. Once you get there, death, murder, disease, destruction, and torment always follow.

Our feet symbolize our lifestyle – how we live our lives. Where are your feet taking you? Where are you going?

Rather than running to evil, we must ask the Lord to lead us to holiness.

He restoreth my soul: he leadeth me in the paths of righteousness for his name's sake. Psalm 23: 3

Teach me thy way, O LORD, and lead me in a plain path, because of mine enemies. Psalm 27: 11

And see if there be any wicked way in me, and lead me in the way everlasting. Psalm 139: 24

Chapter 6: A false witness who speaks lies

There is a difference between telling lies, and being a false witness. In a courtroom, a false witness lies about what he or she has seen. Such lies can result in a wrongful conviction of an innocent person.

Thou shalt not bear false witness against thy neighbour. Exodus 20: 16

This is the ninth commandment. God Himself wrote the commandments on stone tablets, and gave them to Moses to deliver to His people. God could have given Moses a thousand commandments, but he narrowed it down to ten. Not bearing false witness made the top ten! This shows how serious it is to God.

Thou shalt not raise a false report: put not thine hand with the wicked to be an unrighteous witness. Exodus 23: 1

It is a crime to make a false report to law enforcement. No matter how irritating our next-door neighbors may be, we must resist the temptation to make a false report against them.

If a false witness rise up against any man to testify against him that which is wrong; Then both the men, between whom the controversy is, shall stand before the LORD, before the priests and the judges, which shall be in those days; And the judges shall make diligent inquisition: and, behold, if the witness be a false witness, and hath testified falsely against his brother; Then shall ye do unto him, as he had thought to have done unto his brother: so shalt thou put the evil away from among you. Deuteronomy 19: 16 - 19

We see this same principle throughout the Bible. Those who dig a ditch, hoping to see their enemy fall into it, will fall into it themselves (Psalm 7: 15). Those who lay a trap for their enemy will be caught in that same trap (Psalm 9: 16).

Those who bear false witness against someone else will be punished with the same punishment they wanted the other person to have.

Saul bore false witness against David. Saul knew that David had been anointed king, and he was consumed by jealousy. He wanted to remain king forever. He slandered David to his servants and his army.

Then Saul said unto his servants that stood about him, Hear now, ye Benjamites; will the son of Jesse give every one of you fields and vineyards, and make you all captains of thousands, and captains of hundreds; That all of you have conspired against me, and there is none that sheweth me that my son hath made a league with the son of Jesse, and there is none of you that is sorry for me, or sheweth unto me that my son hath stirred up my servant against me, to lie in wait, as at this day? 1 Samuel 22: 7 - 8

All of this was a lie. Saul was telling his servants that as king, he would give them everything, and David would give them nothing. He also lied and said that David had turned Jonathan, Saul's son, against his own father. None of that was true.

Many of the beautiful Psalms that David wrote were born out of the pain his heart felt from the slander Saul had spoken against him.

Deliver me not over unto the will of mine enemies: for false witnesses are risen up against me, and such as breathe out cruelty. Psalm 27: 12

False witnesses did rise up; they laid to my charge things that I knew not. They rewarded me evil for good to the spoiling of my soul. Psalm 35: 11 – 12

***

No one could say anything against Jesus Christ that was true. Since the religious leaders of His day were so determined to destroy Him, they made up things that were not true.

Now the chief priests, and elders, and all the council, sought false witness against Jesus, to put him to death; But found none: yea, though many false witnesses came, yet found they none. At the last came two false witnesses, And said, This fellow said, I am able to destroy the temple of God, and to build it in three days. Matthew 26: 59 - 61

The carnal nature of man will always cause him to look at spiritual things from a natural perspective. Of course, no one could rebuild the physical temple in three days. Because the council could not see the spiritual meaning of Jesus' words, they seized on what the false witnesses said as proof that Jesus was a criminal.

Does saying that a physical temple can be rebuilt in three days warrant a death sentence? Of course not. But the council wanted Jesus dead, so that statement was enough for them.

It's ironic that the false witnesses actually spoke the truth in this case; those who heard it just interpreted it wrongly.

In Leviticus chapter six, we read how God feels about swearing falsely. In verses two through four, an important principle is outlined. If someone you know has given you something of value to keep safe for him, or if you find something that belongs to someone else, or if you get anything by deceit, the Lord expects you to return whatever it is to its rightful owner. Even in our modern day, there are laws against receiving stolen property.

There is a spiritual principle at work here. If you knowingly keep something that belongs to someone else, or receive something that you know was gotten through illegal means, you are a false witness. How so? You are saying (without actually speaking the words), that this item belongs to you, when you know that it doesn't.

And ye shall not swear by my name falsely, neither shalt thou profane the name of thy God: I am the LORD. Leviticus 19: 12

How many times have you heard someone say, "I swear to God," followed by some outlandish statement? The people who say "I swear to God" most often seem to be the ones who also make the most false statements.

God doesn't take this lightly. If you want to be a false witness who speaks lies, that is your choice, but don't drag God into your lies.

Thou shalt not take the name of the LORD thy God in vain; for the LORD will not hold him guiltless that taketh his name in vain. Exodus 20: 7

Taking the Lord's name in vain is not just cursing. It is also swearing that you are about to tell the truth, the whole truth, and nothing but the truth, when in fact you know very well that everything you're about to say is a lie.

Being a false witness misrepresents God. This happens frequently in the church. For example, it is very common for someone to say, "The Lord told me to tell you…" when it is something the Lord did not say at all. Sometimes the guilty party is aware of what she is doing, and sometimes she is genuinely misled.

Often, jealousy is the motive behind this. Some churches are very legalistic, and when someone steps out of line, someone else is quick to bring the hammer down on an unsuspecting brother or sister. If someone's skirt is too short, or heels are too high, or someone hogs the microphone too much, the spirit of jealousy takes over, and that person receives a talking to. This is all cloaked under the mantle of: The Lord said… the Lord wants you to stop… the Lord doesn't like it when you (fill in the blank).

And this is why God hates so much a false witness that speaks lies.

Let's not misrepresent God. We have His word, which is our instruction manual for life, and His word tells us that our witness must be true.

A faithful witness will not lie: but a false witness will utter lies. Proverbs 14:5

Years ago I worked in a bank. We were all required to work one Saturday morning per month. After several months of extremely slow Saturdays, I had a family obligation arise. I asked my supervisor if it was okay if I did not come in on the Saturday I was scheduled to work. He told me that was fine.

On Monday morning, a co-worker pulled me aside. She had witnessed and overheard a conversation between another co-worker, Pat, and our supervisor.

Pat was working the Saturday I had asked off, and noticed that I wasn't there. Bright and early Monday morning, before I arrived, she marched into our supervisor's office with a gleam in her eye, and told him that she felt it was her duty to let him know that I hadn't shown up on Saturday. He let her go on and on – her monologue interspersed with comments like, "I certainly don't want her to get in trouble," and, "I just felt for the good of the office that you should know what happened," etc. My co-worker friend heard everything and was choking back her laughter as Pat "did her duty." Finally, when Pat paused for breath, our supervisor told her that I had asked for the day off, and he had given it to me. Pat sat stunned for a moment, then got up and left his office silently.

When I came in a few minutes later, I overheard Pat say loudly to another co-worker that she had a headache, and was going home. I think it would be more accurate to say that her headache was named Julia, and the headache had just walked in the door.

At the time that this happened, I was very indignant and disgusted with Pat. After all these years, I now laugh about it.

A false witness enjoys getting other people in trouble. A false witness lays the blame at an innocent person's feet, then sits back and smiles as that person suffers. In Pat's case, her false witness backfired in a spectacular fashion.

Notice that what Pat had said was actually true! I hadn't shown up for work. But the "false witness" part of her statement lay in the motive and the attitude that she displayed to our supervisor. She said she didn't want me to get in trouble, when in fact that's exactly what she was hoping for.

For out of the heart proceed evil thoughts, murders, adulteries, fornications, thefts, false witness, blasphemies... Matthew 15: 19

Pat resigned shortly after this incident. I hope that was the end of her career as a false witness.

***

Jesus told us that we are actually blessed when people falsely accuse us.

Blessed are ye, when men shall revile you, and persecute you, and shall say all manner of evil against you falsely, for my sake. Matthew 5: 11

Another verse that deals with this is:

Having a good conscience; that, whereas they speak evil of you, as of evildoers, they may be ashamed that falsely accuse your good conversation in Christ. 1 Peter 3: 16

These verses have to do with people falsely accusing you because you are a Christian. These false accusations take many forms, such as:

"You think you're better than everyone else."

"You spend all your time in church – what a waste of time!"

"You're a bigot/ homophobe/ transphobe/ racist because you're a Christian."

Personally, I have had all of these false accusations thrown at me. Rather than live and let live, these false accusers can't stand the Christian lifestyle, and therefore have to come up with lies to accuse those of us who love Jesus.

Think about it: if you spent most of your time drinking in the bar, or gambling in the casino, who would criticize you? Most people would simply say, "You do you," even if they disapproved.

The word "conversation" in 1 Peter 3: 16 means the way you conduct yourself, or your lifestyle. When I turned my life over to Jesus, the things I used to enjoy doing no longer had any appeal. And even though I didn't go around lecturing people who lived a different lifestyle, I didn't have to. The light of Christ shone through my sinful human flesh, and was apparent to everyone – not because I am somehow more special or holy than anyone else (I'm not), but because He is light! The light drew some people to me, and was repelled others.

And this is the condemnation, that light is come into the world, and men loved darkness rather than light, because their deeds were evil. John 3: 19

Don't make the mistake of becoming a false accuser yourself. You absolutely must not and cannot expect a non-Christian to behave like a Christian. What you must do is show love and compassion to that person, pray for him or her, and allow the Holy Spirit to work through you to bring that person to Christ.

Or do you despise the riches of His goodness, forbearance, and longsuffering, not knowing that the goodness of God leads you to repentance? Romans 2: 4 (New King James Version)

God's goodness leads sinners to repentance! Not lecturing, not shaming, not a holier-than-thou attitude, and not false accusations. Remember, a non-believer is drowning in sin and can barely keep his head above water, just as you and I were before Jesus saved us.

Let's be a true witness for Him.

A true witness delivereth souls: but a deceitful witness speaketh lies. Proverbs 14: 25

Chapter 7: One who sows discord among brethren

I could write an entire, separate book about the people who work to separate friends from one another, who actively engage in strategic gossip designed to pit people against each other, and who infiltrate churches with the sole purpose of destroying them. I wish I could say that I am exaggerating, but I am not.

In the parable of the wheat and the tares (Matthew 13: 24 – 30), Jesus tells us that the children of the devil and the children of God grow together side by side (verse thirty eight). Sometimes they are almost indistinguishable from one another. It's hard to grasp that Satan's agents are in the church, but that is actually their favorite place to be.

In the church I grew up in, a person who was extremely misguided destroyed a longtime friendship between two other people. The two friends were an older man, and a much younger man. For whatever reason, they hit it off and got along very well. The older man was a bit of a grump, who most often didn't have much good to say about anything. The younger man was a very encouraging person, who came alongside the grump and modeled positive behavior to him. As the saying goes, opposites attract.

One day, the older man said something negative about the younger man, to a third person. This was not surprising, since most of what he said at any given time was negative. But, the third party rushed to tell the younger man exactly what was said.

Why? What possible good could come of that?

The younger man also rushed. He rushed back to the older man and confronted him. And just like that, their friendship was destroyed. The younger man was willing to forgive and talk it out, but the older man's pride had been affronted, and he refused.

Also take no heed unto all words that are spoken; lest thou hear thy servant curse thee: For oftentimes also thine own heart knoweth that thou thyself likewise hast cursed others. Ecclesiastes 7: 21 - 22

This is why we have to be so careful about what we say! Our ungodly words will always come back to bite us - always.

But I say unto you, That every idle word that men shall speak, they shall give account thereof in the day of judgment. Matthew 12: 36

It breaks my heart to this day when I think about what happened to these two friends. The older man was a nominal Christian, but he could have been mentored and matured by the younger man, who in fact was doing just that, before Satan sneaked in and terminated the process.

To add insult to injury, the third party never admitted any wrongdoing. It makes me wonder if his intention all along was to destroy the relationship.

Where no wood is, there the fire goeth out: so where there is no talebearer, the strife ceaseth. Proverbs 26: 20

Why is this going on in the church? Why do people want to destroy friendships?

Again, jealousy is a factor here. If I can't have you as my friend, then he/she can't have you, either.

Another way to sow discord is to meddle in other people's business. In my church, we had someone who told the media people how to run the sound system. She told the children's teacher how to teach the children. She told the cleaning lady how to clean the building. She told the preacher how to preach.

This individual was not interested in genuinely helping out in any of these ministries. Real help is always needed and always appreciated in churches. Rather, she just enjoyed agitating people, with the intention of getting them to leave. Many did.

The worst case I have seen was an individual who had an extremely controlling personality. I accidentally walked into a room where a meeting was being held that I hadn't known about, and I overheard her telling the group what clothes they should wear on the following Sunday. After I picked my jaw up off the floor, I quietly exited the room. Most of the people in that group also ended up leaving the church.

Sometimes, discord is sown unintentionally, but it is still discord. I shake my head when I think about an enthusiastic young man who swept into our church one day. After the service was over, he approached our pastor and began rattling off all of the things that were "wrong" in the sanctuary. He asked for the church credit card, and said he was going to go out and buy new curtains, new microphones, a new podium, etc., etc.

This was the first time he had attended our church.

When I heard this story, weeks later, I felt extreme indignation. First of all, who would hand over his credit card to a stranger? Secondly, why not get to know the church, become a part of it, and find a place to minister effectively? Thirdly, rather than pointing out minor cosmetic flaws, why not thank the Lord for everything that is right about the church?

I must confess I felt some discord within me after this incident. The young man soon moved out of state, presumably to attend a church that was properly accessorized.

Discord is contagious, like a disease.

Another parable spake (Jesus) unto them; The kingdom of heaven is like unto leaven, which a woman took, and hid in three measures of meal, till the whole was leavened. Matthew 13: 33

Leaven (yeast) in the Bible symbolizes evil.

Your glorying is not good. Know ye not that a little leaven leaveneth the whole lump? Purge out therefore the old leaven, that ye may be a new lump, as ye are unleavened. For even Christ our passover is sacrificed for us: Therefore let us keep the feast, not with old leaven, neither with the leaven of malice and wickedness; but with the unleavened bread of sincerity and truth. 1 Corinthians 5: 6 - 8

Gossiping, whispering, complaining, backstabbing, and discontentment are the "leaven of malice." They can spread through the church like wildfire, and they are every bit as destructive.

And this is why God hates so much the one who sows discord among brethren.

The best way to deal with this behavior is to bring it out into the open. When someone starts whispering to you her complaints about the church, stop her from continuing. Grab the pastor or an elder, then tell her to go on with her story in front of that person. This will almost always put a stop to the discord. Of course, the complaining person will then no longer want to be your friend, in which case you should congratulate yourself on shedding that unnecessary baggage.

***

When Mary poured perfumed oil on Jesus, shortly before His crucifixion, one individual didn't like it. He began trying to stir up discord among the disciples.

Then took Mary a pound of ointment of spikenard, very costly, and anointed the feet of Jesus, and wiped his feet with her hair: and the house was filled with the odour of the ointment. Then saith one of his disciples, Judas Iscariot, Simon's son, which should betray him, Why was not this ointment sold for three hundred pence, and given to the poor? This he said, not that he cared for the poor; but because he was a thief, and had the bag, and bare what was put therein. John 12: 3 - 6

Two of the other gospels state that more than one person was upset about this incident.

But when his disciples saw it, they had indignation, saying, To what purpose is this waste? Matthew 26: 8

And there were some that had indignation within themselves, and said, Why was this waste of the ointment made? Mark 14: 4

It is my belief that Judas alone brought up the issue of waste, and in so doing stirred up some of Jesus' other disciples to also be upset about it. Thankfully Jesus corrected them.

Years ago, I had a boss who loved to stir up trouble among his staff. He would make a seemingly innocent, yet very calculated remark, which would cause one person to start thinking negatively about another person in the department. For him, it was entertainment, and he enjoyed watching the chaos that ensued. I fell for it more than once, until I finally wised up and quit listening to his "innocent" remarks.

A naughty person, a wicked man, walketh with a froward mouth. He winketh with his eyes, he speaketh with his feet, he teacheth with his fingers; Frowardness is in his heart, he deviseth mischief continually; he soweth discord. Therefore shall his calamity come suddenly; suddenly shall he be broken without remedy. Proverbs 6: 12 – 15

If you deliberately try to stir up trouble, the Bible says you will be broken without remedy.

Don't do it!

Chapter 8: The body, redeemed

Let's take another look at these verses. I see something fascinating here.

These six things the LORD hates,
Yes, seven are an abomination to Him:
A proud look,
A lying tongue,
Hands that shed innocent blood,
A heart that devises wicked plans,
Feet that are swift in running to evil,
A false witness who speaks lies,
And one who sows discord among brethren.
Proverbs 6: 16 – 19 (New King James Version)

What struck me as I re-read these verses is the fact that we can use our bodies for things that God hates!

Our eyes look at others proudly.

We use our tongues to tell lies.

We use our hands to kill innocent people.

Our hearts are the source of wickedness.

We use our feet to run to do evil things.

And our whole bodies can be used for false witnessing, and for sowing discord.

What? know ye not that your body is the temple of the Holy Ghost which is in you, which ye have of God, and ye are not your own? For ye are bought with a price: therefore glorify God in your body, and in your spirit, which are God's. 1 Corinthians 6: 19 – 20

We are supposed to use our bodies for God's glory, not for doing what He hates.

I started thinking about eliminating from my life the things that God hates, and replacing them with things that He loves.

Compassion instead of pride

Instead of looking down my nose at people, being full of pride, I should look at them with compassion and mercy.

Shouldest not thou also have had compassion on thy fellowservant, even as I had pity on thee? Matthew 18: 33

No human being has the right to be proud about anything. Let's remember where God found us, in our sin, and saved us.

If we say that we have no sin, we deceive ourselves, and the truth is not in us. 1 John 1: 8

Truth instead of lies

It is so tempting to lie. We even rationalize it by telling ourselves we don't want to hurt someone's feelings. But the truth is not only the better choice, it is the only choice.

But speaking the truth in love, may grow up into him in all things, which is the head, even Christ... Ephesians 4: 15

Ask the Lord for wisdom in speaking. He will give you the right words to say at the right time, even in situations where you think a lie is kinder!

Behold, thou desirest truth in the inward parts: and in the hidden part thou shalt make me to know wisdom. Psalm 51: 6

Life instead of death

Even if you don't physically kill someone with your hands, the things that you are doing can lead to someone's death. In the Bible, our hands symbolize our works. If you are campaigning for a political candidate who is pro-abortion, for example, you are using your hands to shed innocent blood.

Lay hands suddenly on no man, neither be partaker of other men's sins: keep thyself pure. 1 Timothy 5: 22

I personally don't buy anything that is made in China, because I know that enslaved people make those items, and many of them are tortured to death by the Chinese communist party when they are no longer considered to be useful.

So shalt thou put away the guilt of innocent blood from among you, when thou shalt do that which is right in the sight of the LORD. Deuteronomy 21: 9

Righteousness instead of wickedness

Righteousness exalteth a nation: but sin is a reproach to any people. Proverbs 14: 34

As hard as it may be, I try to pray for the people who have hurt me. I ask the Lord to correct them and set their feet on the right path. That is His job, not mine.

Dearly beloved, avenge not yourselves, but rather give place unto wrath: for it is written, Vengeance is mine; I will repay, saith the Lord. Romans 12: 19

Good instead of evil

Wouldn't it be great if people were quick to run to do good to other people, instead of being so quick to run to do evil?

Knowing that whatsoever good thing any man doeth, the same shall he receive of the Lord, whether he be bond or free. Ephesians 6: 8

As Christians, we know that our good works won't earn us a place in heaven, but personally, I am overjoyed at the thought that whatever good I do manage to do, God will give the very same thing back to me.

Let your light so shine before men, that they may see your good works, and glorify your Father which is in heaven. Matthew 5: 16

Witnessing for Christ instead of the devil

It has been said that you and I are the only Bible a non-believer may ever read. What do people see when they look at our lives? Do our lives show a true witness for Jesus Christ?

And this gospel of the kingdom shall be preached in all the world for a witness unto all nations; and then shall the end come. Matthew 24: 14

If we live our lives for Jesus Christ, we often don't even have to speak a word to others. They will look and see that Jesus lives in us, that we are different from the rest of the world.

To whom God would make known what is the riches of the glory of this mystery among the Gentiles;

which is Christ in you, the hope of glory... Colossians 1: 27

Harmony instead of discord

How much better the world would be if people would work to unite one another, instead of dividing one another! Today it seems that almost everyone identifies him- or herself by race, political party, gender, or some other subgroup. I am a child of the Most High God! That is the only group I want to be a part of.

Blessed are the peacemakers: for they shall be called the children of God. Matthew 6: 9

We all have much more in common with one another than we think. We are all sinful human beings. We all need a savior.

And all things are of God, who hath reconciled us to himself by Jesus Christ, and hath given to us the ministry of reconciliation... 2 Corinthians 5: 18

The whole world is waiting for the manifestation of the sons of God.

For the earnest expectation of the creature waiteth for the manifestation of the sons of God. Romans 8: 19

When God changes us in a moment, in the twinkling of an eye (1 Corinthians 15: 52), we will be perfectly conformed to the image of Jesus Christ. We will be changed, and the world will be changed!

For we know that the whole creation groaneth and travaileth in pain together until now. And not only they, but ourselves also, which have the firstfruits of the Spirit, even we ourselves groan within ourselves, waiting for the adoption, to wit, the redemption of our body. Romans 8: 22 - 23

Our sinful, corrupt bodies will be redeemed! We will be like Jesus Christ. We will no longer use our bodies to do things that God hates. I don't know about you, but I am excited about that.

***

Abhor that which is evil; cleave to that which is good. Romans 12: 9b

I trust that this book has blessed you. It has blessed me as well! Please visit our website for more resources:

www.giantpublishingcompany.com

www.ingramcontent.com/pod-product-compliance
Lightning Source LLC
Chambersburg PA
CBHW050653160426
43194CB00010B/1920